This edition OP

Various PODs available

TORPEDO WAR,

AND

SUBMARINE EXPLOSIONS

BY

ROBERT FULTON

FELLOW OF THE AMERICAN PHILOSOPHICAL SOCIETY
and of the
UNITED STATES MILITARY AND PHILOSOPHICAL SOCIETY

A Reproduction

ROBERT FULTON

THE **SWALLOW PRESS** INC.
CHICAGO

Published by
The Swallow Press Incorporated
1139 South Wabash Avenue
Chicago, Illinois 60605

INTERNATIONAL STANDARD BOOK NUMBER 0–8040–0533–8
LIBRARY OF CONGRESS CATALOG CARD NUMBER 73–150760

CONTENTS

FOREWORD

In nearly all research libraries, a portion of the collection —sometimes large, usually small—is stored safely away from casual use and viewing. This practice is not entirely due to perverse "librarianship," but to insure preservation for scholarly use or because of monetary value or fragility.

Unfortunately, many fascinating works are thus unknown by those who enjoy beautiful graphics and intriguing texts. While the scholar may track down the important edition, or the curator occasionally expose text or illustration to public exhibition, there is still not opportunity for wide acquaintance and personal enjoyment.

As a small remedy, The John Crerar Library sponsors a series, "Crerar Classics," reproduced from its collections. Candidate works are selected by reason of historical importance, engaging content, or graphic excellence. These are issued in various forms appropriate to the conditions of the original publication, to make possible the leisurely savoring of text or artistry and the joys of personal ownership.

WILLIAM S. BUDINGTON
Executive Director and Librarian
The John Crerar Library

INTRODUCTION

One of Robert Fulton's biographers gave as justification for adding to the number of previous biographies that "not one of them is altogether fair and impartial. Fulton's American biographies have credited him with greater achievements than the facts warrant, while English writers too often have dismissed him contemptuously as a charlatan, a filcher of other men's brains, or even as a traitor."[1] Dickinson briefly characterizes him as follows:

"Fulton was, if anything, cosmopolitan; born a British subject in a British colony, the seed-time of his life was spent in England, the fruition took place in France, and the harvest was reaped in his native America," the harvest being "the introduction of navigation by steam on a commercial basis in the Western hemisphere."[2]

Robert Fulton was born in Pennsylvania on November 14, 1765, in Little Britain Township, later renamed Fulton Township in his honor. His father, Robert Fulton, Sr., died when Robert, Jr., was three years old. His formal education was limited, and in 1782, at the age of seventeen, he moved to Philadelphia. There, by the time he was twenty, he had gained some success as a painter of miniatures. One of his subjects was Benjamin Franklin. With a letter of introduction from Franklin to their fellow American, Benjamin West, in London, Fulton went to England soon after his twenty-first birthday. Benjamin West was already well established as an artist in London, and Fulton profited by his influence and sponsorship. His career as an artist, however, was short-lived, for by 1793 his attention had turned to engineering.

For a period of five years or more, his principal interest was the construction of canals and design of equipment to aid in canal transportation, including boats propelled by steam engines. While he was a follower rather than leader in these early years, he did display great ingenuity, particularly in the practical application of ideas. In 1796, he published two pamphlets, *A Treatise on the Improvement of Canal Navigation* and *Report on the Proposed Canal Between the Rivers Heyl and Helford*. Both exist today in what are probably unique copies. His promotion of small canal construction in England being of small success, late 1797 found him in Paris making attempts to promote their construction in France.

It was during his French period, late 1797 until early 1804, that he became actively engaged in the design and promotion of submarines and underwater explosions. He developed the design, constructed, and tested, with some success, his "plunging boat," the *Nautilus*. After long and fruitless negotiations with the rising Napoleon Bonaparte,

[1] H. W. Dickinson, *Robert Fulton: Engineer and Artist, His Life and Works* (London, New York: John Lane; Toronto: Bell & Cockburn, 1913), vii.

[2] Ibid.

he abandoned all hope of having the boat adopted by France for use against the British navy.

Initially Fulton had invested deep hopes in the French revolution. He saw in the new France a realization of his republican ideals—freedom for men, freedom of trade, freedom of the seas, world peace—and offered his services to France in this cause. England was the villain:

> It is the naval force of England that is the source of all the incalculable horrors that are committed daily. . . .
>
> If by means of the Nautilus one could succeed in destroying the English navy, it would be possible with a fleet of Nautilus to blockade the Thames to the end that England would become a republic. Soon Ireland would throw off the yoke and the English monarchy would be wiped out. A rich and industrious nation would then increase the number of republics of Europe and this would be a long step toward liberty and universal peace.[3]

Fulton's dreams, however, were shattered. Within a few years he was writing about "the tyrannic principles of Bonaparte, a man who has set himself above all law," and about Bonaparte's "insatiable ambition and extravagant ideas."[4]

Fulton then turned to negotiations with the British government. After receiving some assurances of interest, he went to London in April of 1804. The following month his altered allegiance was clear:

> I beg leave to propose one [plan] which will be prompt in execution and if successful will forever remove from the mind of man the possibility of France making a descent on England. I propose a submarine expedition to destroy the fleets of Boulogne and Brest as they now lie.[5]

The following year such an attack was made upon the harbor at Boulogne, though using only Fulton's torpedoes or mines, not his "plunging boat." The mission was a failure. Later that year Fulton successfully demonstrated his torpedo by blowing up the British ship *Dorothea*, described on pages 5–7 of *Torpedo War and Submarine Explosions* (illustration, Plate I). Within a week, however, Admiral Nelson, in conventional naval warfare, destroyed the French and Spanish fleets at Trafalgar, thus undermining England's interest in Fulton and his submarines and torpedoes.

During his two-and-one-half years in England, Fulton prepared detailed drawings and descriptions of a submarine and submarine bombs. These were filed away in archives and not brought to light until early in this century. Fulton's manuscript shows that he foresaw the potentialities of the submarine and the marine mine that were not fully realized until World War I, more than a century later.

These papers also furnish us with a glimpse of Fulton as he refocused his hopes on the homeland

3 William Barclay Parsons, *Robert Fulton and the Submarine* (New York: Columbia University Press, 1922), 32.

4 Ibid., 86, 102.

5 Ibid., 81.

from which he had been gone almost twenty years, and with a summary of his cherished ideas and ideals and his twofold approach to realization of world peace.

Having contemplated the federal government of the United States, the vast country comprised in them which gives room for 120 million inhabitants, seeing the rapid increase of their population and consequently of their industry and commerce, a people without colonies and who did not desire to have any, without enemies on their frontiers, and having nothing to contend for but a rational intercourse with foreign nations by sea, which intercourse would be interrupted by every war which might take place between England and France or between European nations and cause vexatious feuds and parties in America, which might lead to marine and army establishments, to alliances offensive and defensive with European states, thereby directing the ambition of individuals to military fame and the people to warlike pursuits and all their complications of evil, which might finally divide the states and destroy a system which should progress *as near as man is capable* to the perfection of civilization:

It was to prevent the possibility of all such consequences, by destroying the principles which lead to them, that induced me at first to contemplate a plan which might destroy all military marines and give liberty to the seas. . . .

What I mean by the liberty of the seas is that all vessels of all nations should carry any kind of cargo to any port of any and every nation wherever the owners thought proper to send them. . . . Under such a system, infinite stupid causes of war will be done away, and the genius and millions which are now expended on wars will then be directed to useful enterprises. . . .

I therefore looked to the arts for efficient means, and after some months study found that only two things were wanting: First to navigate under water, which I soon discovered was within the limits of physics. Second, to find an easy mode of destroying a ship, which after a little time I discovered might be done by the explosion of some pounds of powder under her bottom.[6]

In October 1806, Fulton left England for America. Within a month of his arrival in the United States, he was proposing to the government demonstrations of his torpedoes. In January 1807, he made a presentation to Secretary of State James Madison and to Secretary of the Navy Robert Smith. Two months later he wrote about his "preparing the engines for an experiment of blowing up a vessel in the harbour of New York this Spring. . . . I hope to convince the rational part of the inhabitants of our cities that vessels of war shall never enter our harbours or approach our Coasts but by our consent."[7] This is the demonstration Fulton describes on page 7 of *Torpedo War*. American response was not enthusiastically favorable.

6 Ibid., paragraphs 1, 2, 4: 54-55; paragraph 3: 142-43. Italics are Fulton's. Spelling and punctuation have been modernized. (H.H.H.) .

7 Alice Crary Sutcliffe, *Robert Fulton and the "Clermont"* (New York: The Century Company, 1909), 288.

However, British interest in Fulton's work revived. In 1807, Lord Stanhope secured a patent on ship-building improvements for "counteracting or diminishing the danger of that most mischievous invention for destroying ships and vessels known by the name or appelation of Submarine Bombs, Carcasses, or Explosions."[8] Also, in the same year, Commodore Owen, who had been associated with Fulton when Fulton was in England, furnished the Admiralty with suggestions for defense against the torpedo; these were forwarded to the British admiral in command of the American station.

Fulton continued efforts to get his torpedo adopted. 1810 witnessed his greatest success. In January of that year, he published *Torpedo War*. This helped implement a proposal of four years earlier: "It is my intention to give this system to the public engraved with every necessary detail."[9] In February of 1810, his offer to exhibit a working model to Congress (see page 10 of *Torpedo War*) was brought up in the legislative hall, but permission was denied. Nevertheless, in March, $5,000 was authorized for "trying the practical use of the torpedo."[10] In May, Secretary of the Navy Paul Hamilton appointed a seven-man committee to view and evaluate Fulton's experiments.

Cadwallader D. Colden, lay scientist and district attorney of New York City, would be, in seven years, Fulton's first biographer. John Kemp was professor of mathematics and geography at Columbia College in New York City. Morgan Lewis had recently completed a term as governor of New York. Robert R. Livingston, when U.S. Minister to France during the period 1801–04, had encouraged and financed Fulton's work on the submarine in that country. Colonel Jonathan Williams was the first superintendent of West Point. Oliver Wolcott was a New York City businessman and former Secretary of the Treasury, having succeeded Alexander Hamilton. John Garnett completed the committee.

From September 21 through November 1, meetings and experiments were conducted in and around New York City. During December 1810 and January 1811, the committee, and the naval officers involved, submitted their judgments. Commodore John Rodgers had rigged one ship with nets hanging into the water around its circumference. Fulton, surprised, admitted that this defense foiled his torpedoes, though he was certain he could surmount the difficulty, if indeed the cumbersomeness of the netting device itself did not render the ship too unmaneuverable. In Commodore Rodgers' journal report, the repetition of the phrase, "calculated to supercede the necessity of a navy," characterizing Fulton's project, seemed to indicate the fear of any naval officer. Rodgers was presumably happy to report negatively on the outcome of Fulton's demonstrations. Even when Fulton's cable-cutting device worked, Rodgers

---

8 Dickinson, *Robert Fulton*, 208.

9 Parsons, *Robert Fulton*, 142.

10 *American State Papers: Documents, Legislative and Executive, of the Congress of the United States*. (Washington: Gales & Seaton, 1834), Class VI: Naval Affairs, 234.

judged that "I, nevertheless, deny that it is possible to use this machine so as to make it of any importance as an engine of war."[11] He concluded his report with these words:

> Mr. Fulton has pledged himself . . . to acknowledge in a public manner the incorrectness of all such part of his theory as he should not be able to establish by these experiments; consequently I cannot but conclude that . . . [he will] publish to the citizens of the United States, in the same public manner, that what he may have led them to expect he now finds himself unable to perform, namely, that his torpedoes . . . were . . . comparatively of no importance at all.[12]

Messrs. Garnett, Kemp, Williams, and Wolcott judged Fulton's experiments inconclusive. Future improvements and demonstrations would have to prove whether torpedoes were a proper "means of public defence."[13]

Messrs. Colden, Lewis, and Livingston were more enthusiastic, though their judgments also rested in the future. Livingston concluded: "I view this new application of powder as one of the most important military discoveries which some centuries have produced."[14] Colden expressed himself similarly: "In time this new application of its [gunpowder] irresistible power, by submarine explosions, may produce greater changes in the world than have been made by it since its introduction into Europe."[15] Lewis: "The experiments . . . warrant an expectation that, aided by Government, (which every practical science promising public utility is entitled to be) and the efforts of genius, the sub-marine use of gunpowder will, at no distant period, be entitled to rank among the best and cheapest defences of ports and harbors."[16]

In February 1811, Fulton submitted a long letter to Secretary Hamilton, summarizing the results of the New York demonstrations and urging continued experiments ($3,500 of the $5,000 budget remained unspent). However, we have no record of further writings or developments by Fulton of his plunging boat or his submarine bombs.

After more than a decade of frustration, Fulton turned his full ingenuity and energies to the development of steamboats, which had occupied some of his attention in both England and France. Here he enjoyed success; but this is another story, and the one for which Fulton is most widely known.

HERMAN H. HENKLE
Executive Director, *Retired*
The John Crerar Library

---

11 Ibid., 242.
12 Ibid., 242-43.
13 Ibid., 235.
14 Ibid., 239.
15 Ibid., 237.
16 Ibid., 239.

TORPEDO WAR,

AND

SUBMARINE EXPLOSIONS.

BY

ROBERT FULTON,

FELLOW OF THE AMERICAN PHILOSOPHICAL SOCIETY,
and of the
UNITED STATES' MILITARY AND PHILOSOPHICAL SOCIETY.

—✦—

The Liberty of the Seas will be the Happiness of the Earth.

—〜〜〜〜—

NEW-YORK:

PRINTED BY WILLIAM ELLIOT, 114 *WATER-STREET.*
....
1810.

TORPEDO WAR, &c.

———❖———

To JAMES MADISON, Esq. President of the United States, and to the Members of both Houses of Congress.

GENTLEMEN,

In January last, at Kalorama, the residence of my friend Joel Barlow, I had the pleasure of exhibiting to Mr. Jefferson, Mr. Madison, and a party of gentlemen from the senate and house of representatives, some experiments and details on Torpedo defence and attack; the favourable impression which the experiments appeared to make on the minds of the gentlemen then present; and my conviction that this invention, improved and practised to the perfection which it is capable of receiving, will be of the first importance to our country, has induced me to present you in the form of a pamphlet a description of my system, with five engravings, and such demonstrations as will give each of you an opportunity to contemplate its efficacy and utility at your leisure; and enable you to form a correct judgment on the propriety of adopting it as a part of our means of national defence. It being my intention to publish hereafter a detailed account of the origin and progress of this invention, and the embarrassments under which I have laboured to bring it to its present state of certain utility; I will now state only such experiments and facts as are most important to be known, and which, proving the practicability of destroying ships of war by this means, will lead the mind to all the advantages which we may derive from it. I believe it is generally known that I endeavoured for many years to get torpedoes introduced into practice in France, and in England; which, though unsuccessful, gave me the opportunity of making numerous very interesting experiments on a large scale; by which I discovered errors in the combinations of the machinery and method of fixing the torpedoes to a ship; which errors in the machinery have been corrected: and I believe I have found means of attaching the torpedoes to a vessel which will seldom fail of success. It is the result of my experience which I now submit to your consideration; and hoping that you will feel an interest in the success of my invention, I beg for your deliberate perusal and reflection on the following few pages. Gentlemen who have traced the progress of the useful arts, know the years of toil and experiment, and difficulties which frequently pass, before the utility and certain operation of new discoveries have been established; hence it could not be expected, that torpedoes should be rendered useful without encountering many difficulties; and I am aware, that in the course of farther essays other difficulties will appear; but from my past experience I feel confident, that any obstacle which may arise can be surmounted by attention and perseverance :---of this gentlemen will be better able to judge, after examining the following facts and details.

PLATE I.

PLATE I

Is a view of the brig Dorothea, as she was blown up on the 15th of Oct. 1805.

To convince Mr. Pitt and lord Melville that a vessel could be destroyed by the explosion of a Torpedo under her bottom, a strong built Danish brig, the Dorothea, burthen 200 tons, was anchored in Walmer road, near Deal, and within a mile of Walmer Castle, the then residence of Mr. Pitt. Two boats, each with eight men, commanded by lieutenant Robinson, were put under my direction. I prepared two empty Torpedoes in such a manner, that each was only from two to three pounds specifically heavier than salt water; and I so suspended them, that they hung fifteen feet under water. They were then tied one to each end of a small rope eighty feet long: thus arranged, and the brig drawing twelve feet of water, the 14th day of October was spent in practice. Each boat having a Torpedo in the stern, they started from the shore about a mile above the brig, and rowed down towards her; the uniting line of the Torpedoes being stretched to its full extent, the two boats were distant from each other seventy feet; thus they approached in such a manner, that one boat kept the larboard the other the starboard side of the brig in view. So soon as the connecting line of the Torpedoes passed the buoy of the brig, they were thrown into the water, and carried on by the tide, until the connecting line touched the brig's cable; the tide then drove them under her bottom. The experiment being repeated several times, taught the men how to act, and proved to my satisfaction that, when properly placed on the tide, the Torpedoes would invariably go under the bottom of the vessel. I then filled one of the Torpedoes with one hundred and eighty pounds of powder, and set its clockwork to eighteen minutes. Every thing being ready, the experiment was announced for the next day, the 15th, at five o'clock in the afternoon. Urgent business had called Mr. Pitt and lord Melville to

London. Admiral Holloway, Sir Sidney Smith, Captain Owen, Captain Kingston, Colonel Congreve, and the major part of the officers of the fleet under the command of Lord Keath were present; at forty minutes past four the boats rowed towards the brig, and the Torpedoes were thrown into the water; the tide carried them, as before described, under the bottom of the brig, where, at the expiration of eighteen minutes, the explosion appeared to raise her bodily about six feet; she separated in the middle, and the two ends went down; in twenty seconds, nothing was to be seen of her except floating fragments; the pumps and foremast were blown out of her; the fore-topsail-yard was thrown up to the cross-trees; the fore-chain-plates, with their bolts, were torn from her sides; the mizen-chain-plates and shrouds, being stronger than those of the foremast, or the shock being more forward than aft, the mizenmast was broke off in two places; these discoveries were made by means of the pieces which were found afloat.

The experiment was of the most satisfactory kind, for it proved a fact much debated and denied, that the explosion of a sufficient quantity of powder under the bottom of a vessel would destroy her.*   There is now no doubt left on any intelligent mind as to this most important of all facts connected with the invention of Torpedoes; and the establishment of this fact alone, merits the expenditure of millions of dollars and years of experiment, were it yet necessary, to arrive at a system of practice which shall insure success to attacks, with such formidable engines.   For America, I consider it a fortunate circumstance that this experiment was made in England, and witnessed by more than a hundred respectable and brave officers of the Royal navy; for, should Congress adopt Torpedoes as a part of our means of defence, lords

---

* Twenty minutes before the Dorothea was blown up, Capt. Kingston asserted, that if a Torpedo were placed under his cabin while he was at dinner, he should feel no concern for the consequence.   Occular demonstration is the best proof for all men.

Melville, Castlereagh, and Mulgrave, have a good knowledge of their combination and effect. Lord Grenville, Earls Gray and St. Vincent*, have on their minds a strong impression of their probable consequences. Sir Home Popham, Sir Sidney Smith, and Colonel Congreve, the latter now celebrated for his ingenious invention of Pyrotecnic arrows or rockets, were my friends and companions in the experiments; they are excellent and brave men, and from my knowledge of those noblemen and gentlemen, and their sentiments on this subject, I can predict that they would feel much disposed to respect the rights, nor enter the waters of a nation who should use such engines with energy and effect.

This fortunate experiment left not the least doubt on my mind that the one which I made in the harbour of New-York in August 1807, would be equally successful. The brig was anchored, the Torpedoes prepared and put into the water in the manner before described; the tide drove them under the brig near her keel, but in consequence of the locks turning downwards, the powder fell out of the pans and they both missed fire. This discovery of an error in the manner of fixing the locks to a Torpedo, has been corrected. On the second attempt, the Torpedo missed the brig; the explosion took place about one hundred yards from her, and threw up a column of water ten feet diameter sixty or seventy feet high. On the third attempt she was blown up: the effect and result much the same as that of the Dorothea before described. About two thousand persons were witnesses to this experiment. Thus, in the course of my essays, two brigs, each of two hundred tons, have been blown up. The practicability of destroying vessels by this means, has been fully proved. It is also proved, that the mechanism will ignite powder at any required depth under water within a given time. It now remains to point out means by which Torpedoes may be used to advantage with the least possible risque to the assailants.

* The morning of my first interview with Earl St. Vincent he was very communicative. I explained to him a Torpedo and the Dorothea experiment. He reflected for some time, and then said, Pitt was the greatest fool that ever existed, to encourage a mode of war which they who commanded the seas did not want, and which, if successful, would deprive them of it.

PLATE II,

Represents the anchored Torpedo, so arranged as to blow up a vessel which should run against it; B is a copper case two feet long, twelve inches diameter, capable of containing one hundred pounds of powder. A is a brass box, in which there is a lock similar to a common gun lock, with a barrel two inches long, to contain a musket charge of powder: the box, with the lock cocked and barrel charged, is screwed to the copper case B. H is a lever which has a communication to the lock inside of the box, and in its present state holds the lock cocked and ready to fire. C is a deal box filled with cork, and tied to the case B. The object of the cork is to render the Torpedo about fifteen or twenty pounds specifically lighter than water, and give it a tendency to rise to the surface. It is held down to any given depth under water by a weight of fifty or sixty pounds as at F: there is also a small anchor G, to prevent a strong tide moving it from its position. With Torpedoes prepared, and knowing the depth of water in all our bays and harbours, it is only necessary to fix the weight F at such a distance from the Torpedo, as when thrown into the water, F will hold it ten, twelve, or fifteen feet below the surface at low water, it will then be more or less below the surface at high water, or at different times of the tide; but it should never be so deep as the usual draught of a frigate or ship of the line. When anchored, it will, during the flood tide, stand in its present position; at slack water it will stand perpendicular to the weight F, as at D; during the ebb it will be at E. At ten feet under water the waves, in boisterous weather, would have little or no tendency to disturb the Torpedo; for that if the hollow of a wave should sink ten feet below what would be the calm surface, the wave would run twenty feet high, which I believe is never the case in any of our bays or harbours. All the experience which I have on this kind of Torpedo is, that in the month of October 1805, I had one of them anchored

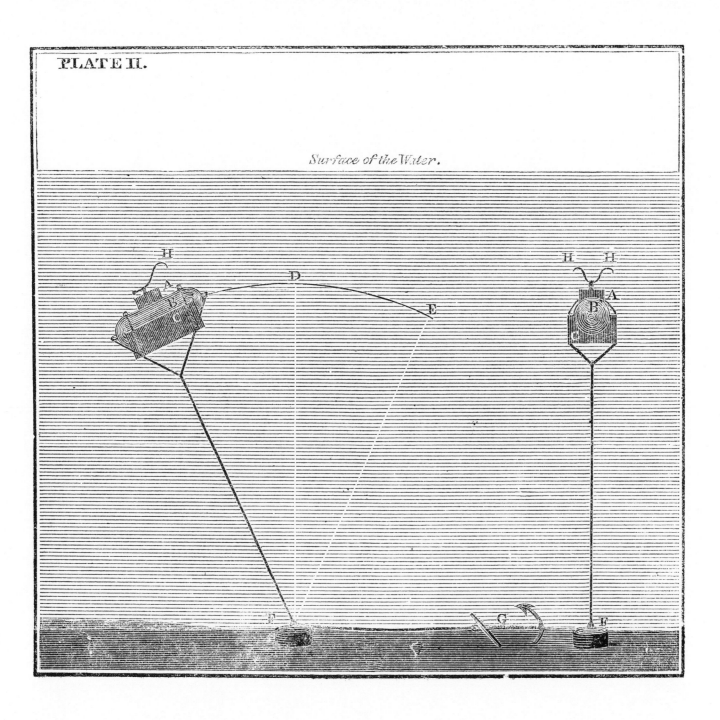

PLATE II.

Surface of the Water.

nine feet under water, in the British Channel near Dover; the weather was severe, the waves ran high, it kept its position for twenty-four hours, and, when taken up, the powder was dry and the lock in good order. The Torpedo thus anchored, it is obvious, that if a ship in sailing should strike the lever H, the explosion would be instantaneous, and she be immediately destroyed; hence, to defend our bays or harbours, let a hundred, or more if necessary, of these engines be anchored in the channel, as for example, the Narrows, to defend New-York.

The figure to the right of the plate is an end view of the Torpedo H. H shews its lever forked, to give the better chance of being struck.

Having described this instrument in a way which I hope will be understood, I may be permitted to put the following question to my readers, which is, knowing that the explosion of one hundred pounds of powder, or more if required, under the bottom of a ship of the line, would destroy her, and seeing, that if a ship in sailing should strike the lever of an anchored torpedo, she would be blown up, would he have the courage, or, shall I say, temerity, to sail into a channel where one or more hundred of such engines were anchored? I rely on each gentleman's sense of prudence and self-preservation, to answer this question to my satisfaction. Should the apprehension of danger become as strong on the minds of those who investigate this subject as it is on mine, we may reasonably conclude that the same regard to self-preservation, will make an enemy cautious in approaching waters where such engines are placed; for, however brave sailors may be, there is no danger so distressing to the mind of a seaman, or so calculated to destroy his confidence, as that which is invisible and instantaneous destruction.

The consideration which will now present itself, is, that the enemy might send out boats to sweep for and destroy the Torpedoes. It is therefore proper to examine the nature of such an operation, and its chance of success. Suppose two hundred Torpedoes to be placed in three miles of channel, the enemy's boats, in attempting to sweep for them, would be exposed to the fire of our land batteries, or necessitated to fight our boats, for whenever they leave their ships and take to boats, we can be as well armed and active at boat fighting as they; and thus opposed by batteries and boats, they would have three or more square miles of channel to sweep, which, even if successful, would be a work of time, and were they to get up some of the Torpedoes, they could not ascertain if all were destroyed, for they could not know whether five or five hundred had been put down; nor could they prevent our boats throwing in additional numbers each day and night. It therefore amounts to an impossibility for an enemy to clear a channel of Torpedoes, provided it were reasonably guarded by land batteries and row boats. Added to the opposition which might be made to the enemy, there is a great difficulty in clearing a channel of Torpedoes with any kind of sweep or drag, so as to establish full confidence in sailing through it. It is only they who put them down and know the number, that could tell when all were taken up. To facilitate the taking of them up, I have, since Plate II was engraved, thought of a very useful and simple piece of mechanism which, being screwed to the box C, will hold the Torpedo under water at any given depth, and for any number of days. They may be set to stay under water a day, week, month, or year, and on the day which shall be previously determined, they will rise to the surface; at the same instant each will lock its lever H so that it cannot strike fire, and the Torpedo may be handled with perfect safety. Not having time to engrave this improvement, it shall be exhibited to Congress in a working model, by which it will also be better understood.

I will now suppose the enemy to be approaching a port; a signal announces them; our boats run out and throw into the channel two hundred Torpedoes, set each to 15 days. Should the enemy sail among them, the consequence will teach future caution; should they cruise or anchor at a distance, what could they do? They not knowing the number of Torpedoes which were put down, nor the day on which they were to rise to the surface, could not have their boats out exposed to our fire, and waiting from day to day for a time uncertain. Whereas, our officers, knowing the number which were put down, and the day they were to rise to the surface, would have their boats ready to take them in, and at the same time replace them with others set for ten, fifteen, twenty, or more days. Viewing this subject in all its bearings, the impression on my mind is, that it would be impossible for an enemy to enter a port where anchored Torpedoes were thus used, without their incurring danger of such a kind, that courage could not guard them from its consequences. Prudence and justice would warrant their abandoning such an enterprise; and the probability is, that knowing us to be thus prepared, they never would attempt it, or should they, and only one vessel were to be destroyed, we might calculate on its good effect to protect us from future hostile enterprises.

PLATE III,

Represents a clockwork Torpedo, as prepared for the attack of a vessel while at anchor or under sail, by harpooning her in the larboard and starboard bow.

B is a copper case to contain one hundred or more pounds of powder; C a cork cushion to give the whole Torpedo such a buoyancy, that it will be only from two to three pounds heavier than salt water. To ascertain such weight, when it is charged with powder and the lock screwed on, it is put into a large tub of sea water. C is to have fifteen or twenty inch-holes bored in its sides and top, to let the water rush in and the air out, otherwise, the air would prevent its immediately sinking. A is a cylindric brass box, about seven inches diameter and two inches deep, in which there is a gun-lock with a barrel two inches long, to receive a charge of powder and a wad, which charge is fired into the powder of the case B. In the brass box A there is also a piece of clockwork moved by a spring, which being wound up and set, will let the lock strike fire in any number of minutes which may be determined within one hour. K is a small line fixed to a pin, which pin holds the clockwork inactive; the instant the pin is withdrawn the clockwork begins to move, and the explosion will take place in one, two, three, or any number of minutes for which it has been set; the whole is so made as to be perfectly tight and keep out the water, although under a pressure of twenty-five or thirty perpendicular feet. D is a pine box two feet long, six or eight inches square, filled with cork; it is ten or fifteen pounds lighter than water, and floats on the surface; the line

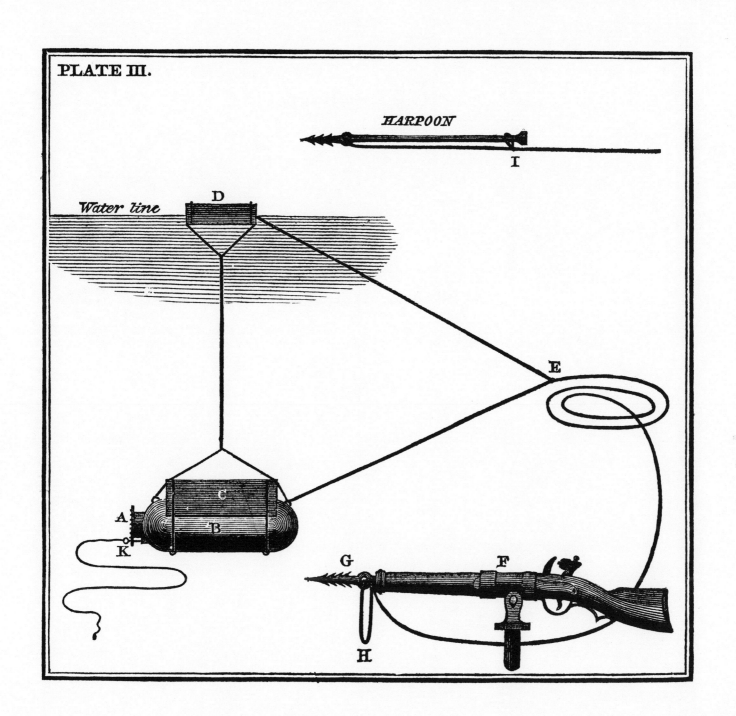

PLATE III.

HARPOON

Water line

from it to the Torpedo is the suspending line, which must be of a length in proportion to the estimated draft of water of the vessel to be attacked; vessels of a certain number of guns usually draw within a few feet of the same draft of water; the suspending line should be from four to eight feet longer than the greatest draft of the vessel, that it may bend round the curve of her side, and lay the Torpedo near her keel. From the Torpedo and the float D, two lines, each twenty feet long, are united at E, from thence one line goes to the harpoon, the total length of the line from the Torpedo to the harpoon being about fifty feet, according to the length of the vessel to be attacked, will, when the ship is harpooned in the bow, bring the Torpedo under her bottom near midship. See the harpoon. It is a round piece of iron, half an inch diameter and two feet long, the butt one inch diameter, the exact calibre of the harpoon gun; in the head of the harpoon there is an eye, the point six inches long is barbed, the line of the Torpedo is spliced into the eye of the harpoon, a small iron or tough copper link runs on the shaft of the harpoon, to the link the Torpedo line is also tied, and at such a distance, that when the harpoon is in the gun it will form a loop as at H, but when fired, the link will slide along to the butt of the harpoon, and, holding the rope and harpoon parallel to each other, the rope will act like a tail or rod to a rocket, and guide it straight; without this precaution, the butt of the harpoon would turn foremost, and make a very uncertain shot. F is the harpoongun, made strong, and to work on a swivel in a stanchion fixed in the stern-sheets of a boat. My experience with this kind of harpoon and gun, is, that I have harpooned a target of six feet square fifteen or twenty times, at the distance of from thirty to fifty feet, never missing, and always driving the barbed point through three inch boards up to the eye, which practice was so satisfactory, that I did not consider it necessary to repeat it. The object of harpooning a vessel on the larboard and starboard bow, is, to fix one end of the Torpedo-line, then, if the ship be under sail, her action through the water will draw the Torpedo under her; if she be at anchor, the tide will drive it under her, where, at the expiration of the time for which the clockwork was set, the explosion will destroy her.

This being the kind of Torpedo and clockwork by which the Dorothea in Walmer roads, and the brig in New-York harbour were blown up, and the harpoon having succeeded to fix the line to the target, these two experiments shall be combined, and the mode of practice, with the prospect of success and risque to the assailants, examined.

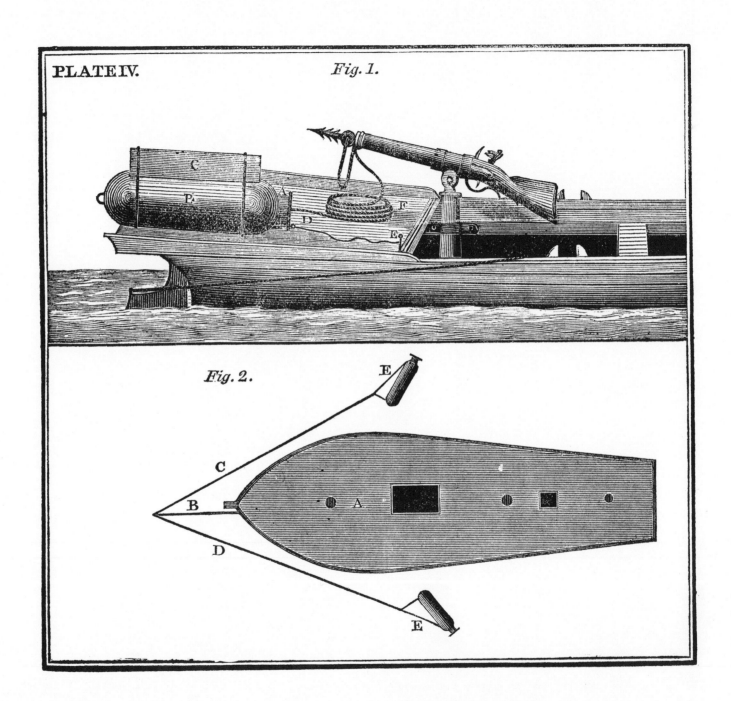

PLATE IV.

Fig. 1.

Fig. 2.

PLATE IV, Fig. 1,

Represents the stern of a row-boat ; a platform about four feet long, three feet wide, is made on her stern on a level with the gunwale, and projecting over the stern fifteen or eighteen inches, so that the Torpedo, in falling into the water, may clear the rudder.   On the platform, the Torpedo and its suspending line of cork are to be laid, and the harpoon-line carefully coiled as at F, so that when the harpoon is fired, the line may develope with ease : very pliable well greased, or white line would be best for this purpose.   The harpoon and gun are so well engraved as require no explanation.   B is the copper case to hold one hundred or one hundred and fifty pounds of powder.   C, the box of cork to diminish its tendency to sink and bring it to a specific gravity of only two or three pounds more than sea-water.   Its suspending box of cork explained in Plate III is not seen in this figure, lest the drawing should be confused ; it can be imagined in its proper place.   A, is the brass box with the clockwork lock ; D, the pin which prevents the clockwork moving ; the line from the pin is tied to a bolt, or otherwise fixed to the boat as at E,   Thus fastened, when the Torpedo is pulled into the water, the pin D will remain in the boat, and the clockwork will begin to act. The man who shall be stationed at the gun, and who may be called the harpooner, is to steer the boat and fire when sufficiently near.   If he fixes his harpoon in the bow of the enemy, it will then only be necessary to row away ; the harpoon and line being fixed to the ship, will pull the Torpedo out of the boat, and at the same instant set the clockwork in motion.   This reduces the attack of each boat to one simple operation, that only of firing with reasonable attention.   Should the harpooner miss the ship, he can save his Torpedo and return to the attack.   While I was with the British blockading fleet off the coast of Boulogne in 1804 and 1805, I acquired some experience on the kind of row-boat best calculated for active move-ments, and which I now believe well adapted to a harpooning and Torpedo attack; hence I propose clink-er-built boats, each twenty-seven feet long, six feet extreme breadth of beam, single banked, and six long oars; one blunderbuss, on a swivel, on the larboard and one on the starboard bow; one ditto on the lar-board and one on the starboard quarter, total four, for which cartridges should be prepared, each containing twelve half ounce balls. To work the blunderbusses, in case of need, two mariners should be placed in the bow, two in the stern; each of those men to be provided with a horse-pistol and cutlass, and each oars-man a cutlass, in case of coming to close quarters with a boat of the enemy.

Total of boat's crew.

1 Harpooner.

1 Bowman.

4 Marines.

6 Oarsmen.

Total 12 Men.

Such boats would be active well armed, and, if good men, may be said to be strong handed, and well prepared to make good a retreat, or act on the defensive, in case of encountering the enemy's boats.

Fig. 2.

A, is a bird's eye view of a vessel at anchor; B, her cable; E E, two Torpedoes; C D, is their coupling line, about 120 feet long; it is here represented touching the cable colapsing, and the Torpedoes driving by the tide under the vessel. This is the manner in which the Dorothea in Walmer roads, and the brig in New-York harbour, were blown up.

PLATE V. *Fig.* 1.

A shews a Torpedo, with the harpoon-line fixed to the centre of its end; when the line is thus fixed, the tide cannot drive the Torpedo under a vessel, for the pressure of the current being equal on both sides, it will hang perpendicular to its suspending box of cork C, Fig. 2, and remain as at B, where, exploding, it would blow the water perpendicular to C, and up the side of the ship; the lateral movement of the water from B to E would give her a sudden cant to one side, but do her no injury. This has been proved by the following practice.

On the first of October, 1805, captain Siccombe, in a galley with eight men and his coxswain, placed two Torpedoes in the manner described, Plate IV, Fig. 2, between the buoy and cable of a French gun-brig, in Boulogne roads. The tide drove them until they both lay perpendicular to her sides. When the French saw captain Siccombe advancing without answering the countersign, they exclaimed that the infernal machines were coming, and fired a volley of musketry at his boat, but without touching a man.* The moment the French fired, fearing the effect of the explosions, they all ran aft and were in the greatest confusion. The tide drove captain Siccombe's boat so far down, that he was obliged to cross under the brig's stern, where, seeing her men collected, and expecting another volley, he discharged at them two blunder-

---

* They had got some idea of these machines, from an attempt which had been made with them against the Boulogne flotilla, in Oct. 1804, called the Catamaran expedition.

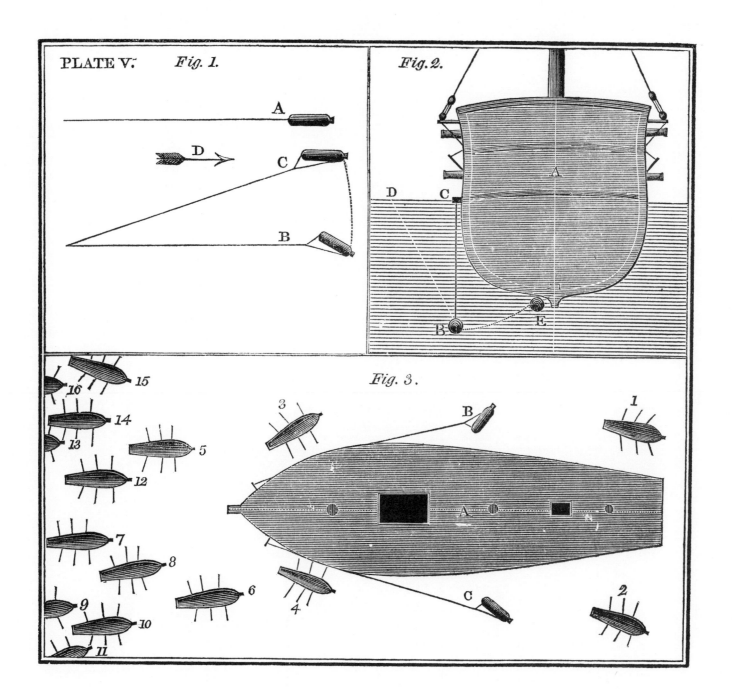

PLATE V. *Fig. 1.*

Fig. 2.

Fig. 3.

busses, each containing fifteen half-ounce balls,* and was rowing away, when both Torpedoes exploded, but, to his astonishment, the brig was not destroyed. On the same night, lieutenant Payne, of captain Owen's ship l'Immortality, placed two Torpedoes across the bow of another French gun-brig; he received their fire, had one man wounded, rowed to some distance, and waited till he saw the explosion of the Torpedoes, which did not appear to do any injury to the vessel. When captain Siccombe called on me in the morning and reported these circumstances, I was much at a loss to account for the brig not being blown up. Defective in the experience which this failure gave me, I had not reflected, that if the copper case, with the clockwork and powder, weighed specifically fifteen or twenty pounds more than water, it would hang like a heavy pendulum to its suspending cork-box C, and if the coupling line were fixed in the centre of the end, as at A, Fig. 1, the action of the tide being equal on both its sides, would have no tendency to sheer or drive it from its perpendicular position. After about half an hour's consideration, I was forcibly impressed with this error in arrangement, as the real cause of captain Siccombe's and lieutenant Payne's failure.

I immediately had a large tub made, then filling a copper case with powder, I screwed on to it the clock-work lock, and tied to it the pine box C, then suspending the whole Torpedo by a line in the tub of sea-water; the end of the suspending line was tied to one end of a scale-beam. I then filled the pine box C with cork, until the whole volume of the Torpedo and box of cork would, when just covered with water, hold three pounds in equilibrio in the scale on the other end of the beam. The Torpedo being then three

* The report on this attack in the French papers, acknowledged that the brig had five men killed and eight wounded: this from two blunderbusses shews that the persons in the vessel attacked have to fear the small arms of the Torpedo boats.

pounds heavier than water, had a sufficient tendency to sink; and being so balanced, would, while under water, be easy moved by a slight pressure to either side. Then, instead of tying the coupling line to the end of the Torpedo, as at A, I tied it to a bridle, as at B, which presenting the side on an angle to the tide, the pressure of the current in the direction of the arrow, would cause the Torpedo to sheer from B to G. This arrangement perfectly succeeded to sheer the Torpedo from its perpendicular C, and the side of the vessel to E, near the keel, a position, near which it should be to do execution. In this situation, the explosion being under the vessel, would have a great body of water to remove laterally, before it could get out by a line curving round her side. The water, when acted on in so instantaneous a manner as by the explosion of one hundred or one hundred and fifty pounds of powder, does, for the instant, operate like a solid body; hence the explosion raises the vessel up with a great force, acting on a small portion of her bottom, which portion giving way, is the same in effect, as though a high sea had lifted her fifteen or twenty feet, and let her down on the point of a rock of three or four feet diameter. This, I believe, accounts for the certain destruction which will follow all explosions that take place near the keel. In all cases when the explosion is under water, the action will be perpendicular to the surface, as from B to C, for in the perpendicular, there are less particles to remove, and less resistance than in any diagonal, as for example, from B to D.

The French papers, giving an account of the attack of captain Siccombe and lieutenant Payne, acknowledged that the Torpedoes blew up along side of the gun-brigs, but gave them only a violent shock and cant to one side; they spoke of the engines as things of little consequence and not to be feared. It is now, however, evident, that they owed the safety of the two brigs to the trifling circumstance of the Torpedoes not being properly balanced in water, and the coupling lines not being tied to a bridle, so as to make the Torpedoes sheer under the bottoms of the brigs.

Fig. 3,

Is a bird's eye view of a ship of the line, either at anchor or under sail, and the Torpedo boats rowing on to the attack. I am sensible that there are strong prejudices against the possibility of row-boats attacking a ship or ships of the line, with any reasonable hope of success; I will, therefore, commence my reasoning and demonstrations by the following questions. What is the basis of the aggression and injustice of one nation towards another? Is it not a calculation on their power to enforce their will? What is the basis of all courage and obstinate perseverance in battle? Is it not a calculation on some real or presumed advantage? A frigate of 30 guns is not expected to engage a ship of eighty guns, for every rational calculation is against her, and to strike her colours would be no dishonour. If I now prove that all the calculations are in favour of the Torpedo boats, it shall hereafter be no dishonour for a ship of the line to strike her colours, and tamely submit to superior science and tactics.

I will run my calculations against a third rate, an 80 gun ship, she being the medium between first rates of 110 guns and fifth rates of 44 guns. I will suppose her to enter one of our ports or harbours in a hostile manner; her draft of water, when loaded, is twenty-two feet; her full complement of men six hundred. Were we to oppose to the enemy an 80 gun ship, she would cost four hundred thousand dollars; we would also have to give her a full complement of six hundred men. If she engaged the enemy, the chances are equal that she would be beaten; if an obstinate engagement, she might have from one to two hundred men killed and wounded, and be so shattered as to require repairs to the amount of forty or fifty thousand dollars; she might be taken and lost to the nation, and add to the strength of the enemy. It is now to be seen if six hundred men and a capital of four hundred thousand dollars, the value of an eighty gun ship, cannot be used to better advantage in a Torpedo attack or defence.

600 men at 12 to a boat, would man 50 boats,

50 boats at one hundred dollars each - - - - - -	$	5,000
50 Torpedoes complete, one hundred and fifty dollars each, powder included		7,500
50 harpoon guns, thirty dollars each - - - - - -		1,500
200 blunderbusses, twenty dollars each - - - - -		4,000
100 pair of pistols, fifteen dollars a pair - - - - -		1,500
600 cutlasses, three dollars each - - - - - - -		1,800
Contingencies - - - - - - - - - -		3,000
Total		24,300

The pay and provisions for six hundred men, whether in an 80 gun ship or in Torpedo boats, may be estimated, for the present, to amount to the same sum annually.

Here is an establishment of fifty boats with their Torpedoes, and armed complete, for 24,300 dollars; the economy 375,700 dollars.* It is evident the ship could not put out fifty boats to contend with our fifty;

* As each boat with a Torpedo, and armed complete, costs four hundred and eighty-six dollars, this economy would pay for seven hundred and eighty-nine boats; hence, eight hundred and thirty-nine Torpedo boats, with Torpedoes and arms, could be fitted out for the sum which one 80 gun ship would cost.

she could not, in fact, put out twenty; therefore, as to boat fighting, the enemy could have no chance of success, and would have to depend for protection on her guns and small arms. Unless in a case of great emergency, the attack should be in the night, for if an enemy came into one of our harbours to do execution, the chances would be much against her getting out and to any great distance before night. In a night usually dark, row-boats, if painted white, and the men dressed in white, cannot be seen at the distance of three hundred yards; and there are nights so dark, that they cannot be seen if close under the bow. I might here draw into my calculations on chances that an enemy, who understood the tremendous consequences of a successful attack with Torpedoes, would not like to run the risk of the night being dark. But in any night, the fifty boats closing on the vessel in all directions, would spread or divide her fire, and prevent it becoming concentered on any one or more boats. Boats which row five miles an hour, and which all good boats can do for a short time, run at the rate of one hundred and forty yards a minute. At the distance of three hundred yards from the ship, they take the risque of cannon shot, which must, from necessity, be random and without aim, on so small a body as a boat, running with a velocity of one hundred and forty yards a minute. At two hundred yards from the ship, the boats must take the chance of random discharges of grape and cannister shot; and at one hundred yards from the ship, they must run the risque of random musket; each boat will, therefore, be two minutes within the line of the enemy's fire before she harpoons, and two minutes after she has harpooned before she gets out of the line of fire, total, four minutes in danger*: the danger, however, is not of a very serious kind, for, as before observed, no aim can

* A deduction may be made from this time; after harpooning, if the ship were anchored in a current which ran one mile and a half an hour, that would be two feet three lines a second; hence, if the distance from the harpoon to the Torpedo were sixty feet, thirty seconds would be sufficient for the tide to push it under the keel; its clockwork might be set to explode in one minute from the time the Torpedo fell out of the boat. If a vessel were under sail, running more than two miles an hour, one minute would be

be taken in the night at such quick moving bodies as row-boats; yet some men might be killed, and some boats crippled†; in such an event, the great number of boats which we should have in motion, could always help the unfortunate. But what would be the situation of the enemy, who had their six hundred men in one vessel? The Torpedo boats closing upon her, twenty-five on the larboard and twenty-five on the starboard bow, some of them would certainly succeed to harpoon her between the stem and main chains, and if so, the explosion of only one Torpedo under her would sink her, killing the greatest part of the people who were between decks, and leave those who might escape to the mercy of our boats to save them.

I now beg of my reader to meditate on this kind of attack, and make up his mind on which are in the greatest danger, the six hundred men in the ship or the six hundred men in the boats? Are not the chances fifty to one against the ship, that she would be blown up before she could kill two hundred men in the boats? Should this appear evident, or be proved by future practice, no commander would be rash enough to expose his ship to such an attack.

To give a fair comparative view of the two modes of fighting, I have, in these calculations, made the number of men on each side equal; by the same rule, if twenty ships of 80 guns were to come into one of our ports, we should be necessitated to have one thousand boats and twelve thousand men; but such a

sufficient time for the clockwork to act before explosion. After explosion there would, of course, be no resistance, and the probability is, that all hands would be too much occupied in attempting to save themselves, to keep them under any discipline. Thus each Torpedo boat would not be more than three minutes within the line of the enemy's fire.

† It is very easy to make the boats so that they cannot be sunk.

preparation would not be necessary.   It can never be necessary for us to have more boats than are sufficient to meet the boats which the enemy could put out to oppose us; an 80 gun ship, which is to work her guns, cannot be encumbered with many boats; they usually have

1 launch, which is a bad rowing boat,

1 long-boat, which may row well,

1 the captain's barge, a good row-boat,

1 yawl or galley, a good row-boat.

They may, in some cases, have two more boats, total number, six; therefore, twelve boats on our part would be sufficient to attack an 80 gun ship*; particularly as all our boats would be built expressly for running, and our business is to run to harpoon and not to fight; for this purpose our six oarsmen, in each boat, never quit their oars, while our four marines keep up a running fire.   The six or eight boats, if the enemy could put out so many, could not prevent our twelve boats closing on the ship.   If our boats came

* While organizing a system of Torpedo attack against the Boulogne flotilla, during the administration of Mr. Pitt, it was determined that men should be taken from Lord Keath's blockading fleet to man the boats; but a difficulty occurred how to carry a sufficient number of good active boats.   Finding that the ships of war could not take on board more than their usual number, without being encumbered, four ordnance vessels were to be prepared, with large hatchways, to receive a number of boats in the hole, and to carry Torpedoes.   Lord Melville was impeached, Mr. Pitt died, and my system was opposed by Lords Grenville and Howic, and the new administration.   I mention this, my experience, to shew that ships of war cannot carry a sufficient number of boats to contend with the boats which we could bring into action; they may, indeed, bring with them ordnance ships to carry boats; but, if they unman the ships to man the boats, the ship will be less formidable in her fire; and I believe it is self-evident, that they who have to cross three thousand miles of sea, cannot be so well furnished with boats as we who command the land.

into contact with the boats of the enemy, the contest would be reduced to boat fighting; the ship could not use her cannon or small arms against us without firing on her own boats. If we succeeded to drive the boats under the guns of the ship, we should follow so close, that her guns and small arms could not be used, for in the night and amidst a number of boats in confusion, they could not discriminate between friends and enemies. On this theory, if twenty ships of 80 guns, or a force to that amount, were to enter one of our ports, two hundred and forty boats, with two thousand, eight hundred and eighty men would be sufficient, and perhaps more than sufficient, for the attack; and the following view of chances exhibits a strong probability, that such a force of Torpedo boats and men would destroy the twenty ships of the line within one hour.

Let the attack be in the night. The enemy must be at anchor; twenty vessels could not keep under way in narrow waters which could not be well known to their pilots. If they put out their boats, they could not bring into action more than six good boats from each ship, total, one hundred and twenty boats. Each ship would be a point from which their boats could depart, or to which they could retreat, total, twenty positions; in these twenty positions, twelve thousand men would be exposed to Torpedo explosion, which is the same, in effect, as a mine under a fortification. We, with two hundred and forty boats, exposing only two thousand, eight hundred and eighty men, would have the whole of our shores to depart from or retreat to; being the assailants, and having it in our power to approach in every direction, the enemy could not know a feint from a real attack, nor could they tell which ship we would attack first; they, consequently, could not concentrate their boats; each vessel would be necessitated to keep her own boats on the look-out, and to aid in protecting her; while we should have the power to divide our force, or concentre one hundred boats on one vessel, as circumstances might require; hence, every thing is in favour of the success of the Torpedo attack, while the greatest danger is to be apprehended for the ships.

Having given my experience and theory on anchored and harpoon Torpedoes: a system, which I hope will, by every friend to America and humanity, be considered of some interest to the United States. I am aware of the doubts which may arise, as to the success of harpooning, in the minds of men in general, and particularly of those who have no experience, who are so impressed with the imaginary tremendous fire of an 80 gun ship, or a ship of war, that the question has often been put to me, where will you find men who have courage to approach in boats within twenty feet of an 80 gun ship, to harpoon her? I answer, that the men in the boats, who are not more than three minutes within the line of the enemy's fire, are not so much in danger, nor does it require so much courage, as to lie yard-arm and yard-arm, as is usual in naval engagements, and receive broadsides, together with grape-shot and volleys of small arms, for forty or sixty minutes. It is not so great a risque, nor does it require so much courage, as to approach a vessel in boats, climb her sides, and take her by boarding, yet this has frequently been done. The risque is not so great, nor does it require so much courage, as to enter a breach which is defended by interior works and close ranges of cannon, flanked by howitzers or carronades loaded with cannister or grape-shot, and the parapet crowded with infantry; yet such breaches have been forced, and cities taken by assault, with numerous examples of this kind. 1 hope there can be no doubt of sufficient courage to make a Torpedo attack. In the instances of captain Siccombe and lieutenant Payne, before mentioned, they considered the risque of so little importance, that they went to the attack without any apparent concern; and the sailors, who were offered a few guineas for each gun of a vessel which they should destroy, used all their influence with the officers to be permitted to be of the party. But I will not propose a project so novel, and look to others to execute it. If Torpedoes be adopted as a part of our means of defence, with a reasonable number of men organized and practised to the use of them, if it be thought proper to put such men under my command, and an enemy should then enter our ports, I will be responsible to my fellow-citizens for the courage which should secure success. While I propose this, I wish it to be understood, that I do not desire any command or public employment. My private pursuits are the guarantee of an independence and freedom of action, which is always grateful to my feelings; they are useful and honourable amusements, and the most rational source of my happiness.

Estimate for an anchored Torpedo.

Thirty-two pounds of copper, at seventy-five cents a pound - - - -	$ 24 00
A lock in a brass box, water-tight - - - - - - - -	20 00
One hundred pounds of powder, twenty cents a pound - - - -	20 00
Machinery to let it rise to the surface in a given time, rope, cork-box, anchor, and weights - - - - - - - - - - -	20 00
Total	84 00

In page 22, I have given an estimate for a clockwork and harpooning Torpedo.

The Torpedo will cost - - - - - - - - - -	150 00
Each boat, armed complete - - - - - - - - -	336 00

Estimate for an establishment in our most important and vulnerable Ports.

	Boats.	Anchored Torpedoes.	Clockwork Torpedoes.
Boston,	150	300	300
New-York,	150	300	300
In the Delaware,	50	200	100
Chesapeake,	100	200	200
Charleston,	100	200	200
New-Orleans,	100	200	200
Total,	650	1400	1300

650 boats, at three hundred and thirty-six dollars each - - - - 218,400 dolls.

1400 anchoring Torpedoes, eighty-four dollars each - - - - 117,600

1300 clockwork Torpedoes, one hundred and fifty dollars each - - 195,000

Total 531,000

Having mentioned the ports in which it is most probable the enemy would attempt to make an impression, calculations can be made for a like mode of defending other situations—a *minutiæ*, which I am not prepared to enter into, nor is it necessary in the present state of this disquisition. I have shewn a strong power, in boats and Torpedoes, to defend six of our principal ports. Gentlemen will please to look to the numbers allotted to each port, and reflect, whether an enemy would not be inclined to respect a force so active and tremendous in its consequences; a force, which under the cover of the night, could follow them into every position within our waters, and pursue them for some leagues from our shores into the open sea;

yet those establishments would not require an expenditure of four hundred thousand dollars; for the cutlasses and fire-arms to arm the boats, and the powder for the Torpedoes, are already in our arsenals and magazines. And what is four hundred thousand dollars in a national point of view? A sum, which would little more than build and fit out for sea two ships of 30 guns. After reflecting on these experiments and demonstrations, I hope no one will, for a moment, hesitate in deciding, that the two thousand, seven hundred Torpedoes and six hundred and fifty boats, before estimated, will be a better protection for six of our sea-ports, than two ships of thirty or any other number of guns. To man the boats in the different ports, nothing more will be necessary than a marine militia; they can be as numerous as any possible necessity could require; and should be exercised to row and use the Torpedoes until the practice became familiar; after which practice, once a month would be sufficient. Corps thus formed, would be no expence to the national government; Torpedoes would require no repairs, and the boats, carefully laid up in houses built for the purpose, would last many years.

To compare Torpedoes with the usual marine establishments, and the superior protection which they give, for any specific sum expended, I have stated this prospect of economy; but I do not consider economy, in the commencement of such a system, as an object of primary importance. Let our fellow-citizens be convinced. Convince the people of Europe of the power and simple practice of these engines, and it will open to us a sublime view of immense economy in blood and treasure. As we are not in actual hostility, and have no opportunity to try experiments on an enemy, my opinion is, that we should immediately prepare for such an event; and to satisfy the public, we should, without loss of time, make the following experiment.

Purchase a strong ship; make six Torpedoes; build two good row-boats, and prepare them as for action, with twelve men each. Let the ship be anchored, and the men practised in harpooning, throwing the Torpedoes, and observing the action of the tide in driving them under her bottom. After practising on her while at anchor, the ship to be got under way in moderate and stiff breezes, and while under way, the men to row at and harpoon her, letting the Torpedoes fall into the water, and observing the action of the current in driving them under her bottom. When the men have been so exercised as to be certain of harpooning the ship, the Torpedoes to be charged, a committee appointed, or the whole of congress witness the effect, the ship to be put under way, the helm lashed, her men take to the boat, the Torpedo boats advance, harpoon her, and blow her up. The success of such an experiment will shew the value of the system; to which courage must be added in case of an actual engagement.

Probable expence of such an experiment.

A strong though old ship - - - - -	1000 dolls.
Six Torpedoes, one hundred and fifty dollars each - -	900
Two boats, one hundred dollars each - - - -	200
Two harpoon-guns - - - - - -	60
Total,	2160

Twenty-four men can be chosen from the sailors in government employ.

THOUGHTS

On the probable effect of this invention.

AT the time a new discovery is made in physics or mathematical science, the whole of its consequences cannot be foreseen. In the year 1330, Bartholomew Schwartz is said to have invented gun-powder; twenty-five years after, a very imperfect kind of cannon was constructed of welded bars of iron, others of sheet-iron, rolled in the form of a cylinder and hooped with iron rings; in some cases, they were made of leather, strengthened with plates of iron or copper; balls of stone were used; and it was not until the beginning of the fifteenth century, that is, one hundred and seventy years after the invention of powder, that iron balls were introduced into practice. Muskets were not used until the year 1521, or one hundred and ninety-one years after the invention of gun-powder. The Spaniards were the first who armed their foot-soldiers in this manner—they had matchlocks; but firelocks, that is, locks with flints, were not used until the beginning of the eighteenth century, one hundred and eighty years after the invention of muskets, and three hundred and eighty years after the invention of powder. When firelocks were first invented, Marshal Sax had so little confidence in a flint, that he ordered a match to be added to the lock with a flint, lest the flint should miss fire*: such is the force of habit and want of faith in new inventions.

---

* I have seen one of these firelocks in the collection of ancient arms, Rue de Bacq. Paris.

Although cannon, fire-arms, and the whole detail of ammunition, now appear extremely simple, yet we here see the very slow advances to their present state of perfection; and they are still improving: hence I conclude, that it is now impossible to foresee to what degree Torpedoes may be improved and rendered useful. When Schwartz invented powder, it may be presumed that his mind did not embrace all its consequences, or perceive that his discovery would supercede the use of catapultas, armour, bows and arrows, and totally change the whole art of war. He certainly could have no conception of such a combination of art as we now see in ships of the line; those movable fortifications, armed with thirty-two pounders, and furnished with wings, to spread oppression over every part of the ocean, and carry destruction to every harbour of the earth. In consequence of the invention of gun-powder, ships of war have been contrived, and increased to their present enormous size and number;* then may not science, in her progress, point out a means by which the application of the violent explosive force of gun-powder shall destroy ships of war, and give to the seas the liberty which shall secure perpetual peace between nations that are separated by the ocean? My conviction is, that the means are here developed, and require only to be organized and practised, to produce that liberty so dear to every rational and reflecting man; and there is a grandeur in persevering to success in so immense an enterprise—so well calculated to excite the most vigorous exertions of the highest order of intellect, that I hope to interest the patriotic feelings of every friend to America, to justice, and to humanity, in so good a cause.

* Compared with existing military marines, I consider all galleys and vessels of war, which were in use previous to the invention of powder, as very insignificant. It is probable that four 74 gun ships in open sea would destroy all that ever existed at any one time.

I have shewn that a ship of 80 guns and six hundred men, could have little chance of resisting fifty Torpedo boats of twelve men each, equal six hundred men. If it can be admitted possible that an 80 gun ship will be necessitated to retreat before fifty boats, she must run so far that the boats cannot follow her, that is, more than eight or ten leagues; therefore, boats could follow a ship over the narrow parts of the Baltic or British channel; but I will confine my remarks to the British channel, between Boulogne and Romney, from Calais to Dover, and from Ostend to the mouth of the Thames. If I can shew that in those waters the British fleets would be compelled to retreat before Torpedo boats or perish, it follows, that they must yield to a like system of attack in every other sea; and the like combination of power which can force them to yield, will act on all ships of war to their total annihilation.

Let the coast of Boulogne be the scene for action; suppose the British to have one hundred ships of 80 guns, or a force to that amount, equal eight thousand guns and sixty thousand men; this is a greater power than ever has been engaged in one action. I have mentioned large ships, because the strength of a fleet depends more on the size of the ships and weight of metal, than on their number; in such case, the line will not be so much extended as if the vessels were smaller and more numerous; the signals can be seen and answered from the extremities of the line with more certainty, and the order of battle can be better kept. The length of a ship, from the point of the bowsprit to the stern, may be estimated at forty fathoms, and the distance between two ships one hundred fathoms, consequently, the one hundred ships would form one line of fourteen thousand fathoms, or twenty-eight-thousand yards, equal to near sixteen miles. Such a line could not see and answer signals from the van and rear to the centre. It could, however, be formed into four divisions of twenty-five ships each, and they again could be subdivided; but the tactics which must be adhered to when two fleets of near equal force engage, will be of little utility when the attack is made by a sufficient number of Torpedo boats.

Estimate of the force to attack so formidable a blockading fleet.

Men, sixty thousand, a number equal to the British; they cannot all be sailors, nor is it necessary they should, but men, who with six weeks exercise can learn to row well, for to row with tolerable dexterity, is all the nautical knowledge required. To divide the sixty thousand men, twelve in a boat, will require five thousand boats, each of which will be so light, that its twelve men can draw it on the beach above high water mark, or on the sands or plane, in a few minutes, or launch it into the water with equal facility.

Manner of arranging the boats until wanted.

A boat being six feet wide and twenty-seven feet long, if a space of twelve feet wide and thirty-nine feet long be allowed for each boat, four hundred and forty of them would range side by side in the distance of one mile, then leaving twelve feet from the stems of the first row to the sterns of the second, and a like space between each line, the five thousand boats could be laid up on a beach or plane one mile long, one hundred and fifty yards wide, and give sufficient room for the men to get at the boats without confusion; this plan would not require the expence of forming a bason or harbour. Thus arranged, each boat with its Torpedo, harpoon-gun, arms, and oars, in their places, and the twelve men in their stations, six on each side of the boat, the whole could be run into the water and manned in an hour, which facility of embarking is of the first importance for rapid movements, and to take advantage of the weather.*

Estimate for the preparations.

5000 boats, one hundred dollars each - - -	500,000 dolls.
5000 Torpedoes, one hundred and fifty dollars each -	750,000
5000 harpoon guns, thirty dollars each - , -	150,000
Total	1,400,000

This is equal to 315,000l. sterling, or about the value of three ships of 80 guns; it is equal to 7,560,000 livres, a sum of little importance to France, it being not equal to the expences of her government for one day; the men she has, and three times the number if required; the powder for the Torpedoes and arms for the men, are in her magazines.

Suppose the boats and Torpedoes prepared, the harpooners exercised, and the men practised to the oars. The intrepidity of the French, in an assault, has been so often proved, that there can be no question as to their courage to rush on to the attack in any case where there is a reasonable hope of success. It is obvious, that the British ships could not put out a sufficient number of boats to oppose five thousand Torpedo boats;

* When the British fleet is becalmed before Boulogne, the French flotilla is becalmed also, and cannot make any advantageous movements. The calms which lay the British fleet under great disadvantage, will give every possible advantage to the Torpedo boats, and will be the most favourable time for the attack.

consequently, they have no other means of resistance than to manoeuvre and defend themselves from their ports and decks, in the best manner they can devise.

It is now necessary, in calculating the chances of success, to examine various modes of attack and defence; I therefore beg of the reader, never to lose sight of the facility with which the whole of the French boats can be run into the water, manned, and ready for action, or again drawn up on the shore, and with how much ease every advantage may be taken of calms and favourable circumstances; he must also separate from his mind the idea of boats attempting to fight ships; such an attempt would be absurd; it is Torpedoes, those instruments of instantaneous destruction, which are to decide the contest; the boats are but the means of harpooning and attaching the Torpedoes to the ships: this is the whole object of the attack.

In defence, it is to be considered by what means a ship or ships could prevent the boats approaching so near as to harpoon them in the larboard and starboard bow, and make good their retreat? I will name the calm months of June, July, and August, as most favourable for the enterprise. Let it be recollected, that in all attacks of this kind, the boats row at the rate of five miles an hour, or one hundred and forty-six yards a minute; at the distance of four hundred and thirty-eight yards or three minutes from the ship, they will risk random round shot*; at two hundred and nineteen yards or one and a half minutes from the ship, they risk one discharge of grape; at one hundred yards or forty seconds from the ship, they risk one volley of small arms, before they harpoon. After harpooning, it is probable the ship's crew would be more

---

* All shot from cannon, carronades, or howitzers, against boats, must be random: a boat is too small and moves too quick to admit of taking aim; and in the night, musket shot will be random also.

occupied about their own safety, than in standing deliberately to fire at the boats. And thus, each boat will not be more than four minutes within the line of the ship's random shot: such rapidity and decision in attack, gives incalculable advantages to the boats.

First mode of attack.

In a calm and usually dark night, the ships at anchor, either in one line or parallel lines, or promiscuously. The Torpedo boats to be formed into divisions, each division to consist of fifty boats, and to attack one ship. Suppose the ships first attacked to be those nearest the land; in a calm they could not get under way, nor could they change their positions; a ship, by having a spring on her cable, might possibly bring her broadside to bear on the boats; but as the fire of the broadside could do little injury until the boats were within four hundred and thirty-eight yards, or three minutes, of her bow, and, as three minutes after coming within the line of fire is to decide the contest, I conceive that her broadside could not protect her; if the boats, at six hundred yards distance, run for her bow, it would be impossible for her to change her position so quick by a spring on her cable, as the boats could change their direction to keep under her bow. If the ships were in one line, and the headmost first attacked, she could receive no assistance from the vessel astern, for she would lie between the stern ship and the boats, and receive the fire which might be directed for them. If the ships lay in several parallel lines, or promiscuously, and the next line were on her larboard, the larboard ship would be distant at least one hundred fathoms, and while the boats were bearing down, might fire broadsides on them when they were at the distance of two hundred yards; but the moment they closed in with the ship she must cease her fire, otherwise she would do more injury to the ship than to the boats;

the larboard ship would, therefore, only have an opportunity to fire two minutes at the boats, in which time, she might possibly discharge two broadsides ; but as the boats could keep in a line with the bow of the vessel attacked, and there is more danger from the larboard or starboard ship than the one attacked, a better mode would be to attack the headmost ship of each line at the same time ; in such case, each ship would be necessitated to reserve her whole fire for her own defence ; she could not assist the next ship, and thus each vessel would be as much exposed and left to her own resources, as though there were not another ship within three leagues of her.   The succeeding ships of the line, or lines, could be attacked in like manner : hence, this mode of attacking any number of vessels with an equal number of divisions of boats, amounts to nothing more than a repetition of an attack with fifty boats on one ship, and it does not appear to me possible, that her fire could repel fifty boats, or prevent them lodging ten, fifteen, or twenty harpoons, if necessary, in her larboard and starboard bow.   I leave to nautical men and experienced commanders, to shew to the public how a ship or ships of war, anchored in a calm as before stated, could resist such an attack, and their total destruction in a few hours.

But commanders, seeing the danger of being becalmed while at anchor, may keep the fleet under way.

Second mode of attack,

In the night, the ships under way, calm, or light breezes of not more than four knots an hour.   Ships of the line, that are under way, seldom approach nearer each other than a cable's length ; this precaution, is to prevent their running foul and causing confusion ; when expecting an enemy of equal force, the custom is to form one line ; admitting, that to oppose the Torpedo boats, they preserved this usual order of battle, close hauled and under easy sail, to let the boats come up, here, as in the case of being at anchor, each ship must apply her whole fire against the division of boats which attack her ; she cannot aid the ship next to her. As the boats, advancing under cover of the night, each division will, in three minutes from the time they arrive within danger of cannon shot, be in with the bow of the destined ship, and fire their harpoons into her. Therefore it appears, that her chance while under way is very little better than when at anchor. If, as the boats advance, a ship turns her bow to meet them, she facilitates their harpooning her. Will any other order of battle than one right line, give more security? Would two, three, or four parallel lines, give better protection? In such case, the line nearest the boats would be attacked first, and the other lines taken in succession. Were the ships to form a crescent, the headmost vessels would be first attacked ; in this form, they might surround a number of boats and get them between two fires ; but whatever situation the boats may be in, after they arrive within the range of grape-shot they can, in a few minutes, be under the bow of the ship, where they will be safe from all fire except small arms ; but to arrive under her bow, amounts to a moral certainty of effecting her destruction. Therefore, with the immense advantage which Torpedoes give to an attack with boats, it is of little consequence whether it be made in the night or day, in a calm or a breeze of from four to six knots. If the ships engage with the boats, their case will be desperate. In all my reflections on this kind of war, I see no chance for their escape other than by retreat ; and the moment English ships of war retreat before Torpedo boats, that moment the power of the British marine is for ever lost, and with it the political influence of the nation.

In this view of chances, I have calculated the number of men in the boats equal to the number in the ships, and estimated five thousand boats to be brought into action; but in all cases when there are sufficient Torpedo boats to drive in the boats of the ships, there will be sufficient to attack the fleet; the one hundred ships could not put six hundred good boats in motion, therefore, one thousand Torpedo boats would suffice for the attack; they could be formed into fifty divisions of twenty boats each; they would have every advantage, in a calm, of directing fifty or one hundred boats against one vessel, while the ships would not have the power to concentrate their fire on the boats; the ships could not be defended, unless there were transports or ordonance vessels expressly for carrying good row-boats, the number of which should be sufficient to repel the Torpedo boats; but if ships can only be protected by boats, it follows, that they will cease to be of use, and the contest for the command of the channel must be decided by boat fighting. In such case, the nation which could put in action the greatest number of boats, and was least dependent on commerce, would have a decided advantage. England is more dependent on commerce than France; her merchant vessels could be attacked, destroyed, and her trade ruined; yet the commerce of France could not be more, nor so much, injured as it is at present. In such an event, England, who has usurped the dominion of the ocean and laid all nations under contribution, would be the most humble supplicant for the liberty of the seas. And then the Emperor of France would have a noble opportunity to display a magnanimity of soul, a goodness of heart, which would add lustre to his great actions, and secure to him the admiration of the civilized world, by granting to so ingenious, industrious, enterprising, and estimable a people, a perfect liberty of commerce.*

---

* A government, and particularly a monarchy or aristocracy, may be in the habitual practice of vice, while the people are in

I have now run this subject to a conclusion, in which I do not hesitate to say, that two thousand Torpedo boats and twenty-four thousand men, would take the command of the British channel from Boulogne to Romney, from Calais, Gravlines, Dunkirk and Ostend, to the mouth of the Thames, and that the command of the commerce of those narrow seas, would command the British nation; but there the power of Torpedo boats must cease—a nation cannot send such boats to sea to depredate on commerce, nor to foreign countries on expeditions of conquest, and therefore the seas must be free.

the habitual practice of virtue. In an aristocracy, where the army, navy, places, and pensions, are in the power of the few, the voice of the people has little or no influence. The genius, industry, and enterprise of the English, have converted a barren island into the most fruitful and beautiful spot on earth; their improvements in the useful arts, have made them the greatest and most useful manufacturing people that ever existed. In proportion as the people, by their industry, increased the riches of the nation, the government found a facility in raising revenue, and have loaded the virtuous people with taxes to the amount of twenty-five or more millions a year, to pay for ruinous wars, the conquest of America, the establishment of the Bourbons, and the balance of Europe.

O N

the imaginary inhumanity of Torpedo war.

IN numerous discussions which I have had on this subject and its consequences, it has been stated, that instead of giving liberty to the seas, its tendency would be to encourage piracy and buccaneering, by enabling a few men in a boat to intimidate and plunder merchant vessels, thereby producing greater evil than the existing military marines. This idea, is similar to one which might have arisen on the invention of muskets, which, giving to an individual the power of certain death at the distance of fifty or a hundred yards, robbers might infest the highways, and from an ambush, shoot the traveller and take his property ; yet there is not so much robbery now as before the invention of gun-powder ; society is more civilized ; it is not so much divided into feuds, or clans, to secrete and protect villainy ; and all civilized society will, in their own defence, combine against the robber, who has little chance to escape. In like manner, as an individual, instigated by revenge, might with an air-gun shoot his neighbour, or by means of gun-powder blow up his barn or buildings ; but society combine against such atrocious acts, and he who would commit them, could have little other prospect before him than the gibbet. In the case of pirates or buccaneers, they could not make a Torpedo without some intelligent workmen, who would be a means of discovery. Were they to take a prize, they must have some port to carry it to, or it could be of no use to them ; were they to plunder a ship, they could not carry much in a Torpedo boat, and the boat must have a port to go to, where neighbours or spectators, observing her suspicious character, would lead to investigation; added to which, pirates are seldom constant in their attachment to each other, and each would suspect the other turning informer. It would be difficult for a Torpedo boat to depart from any port of America, and return without being detected. It is certainly much more easy and secure for an individual to go on the highway and rob, yet how seldom is that done. When nations combine against pirates, there is no reason to fear that individuals can make a bad use of this invention.

But men, without reflecting, or from attachment to established and familiar tyranny, exclaim, that it is barbarous to blow up a ship with all her crew. This I admit, and lament that it should be necessary; but all wars are barbarous, and particularly wars of offence. It is barbarous for a ship of war to fire into a peaceable merchant vessel, kill part of her people, take her and the property, and reduce the proprietor with his family from affluence to penury. It was barbarous to bombard Copenhagen, set fire to the city, and destroy innocent women and children. It would be barbarous for ships of war to enter the harbour of New-York, fire on the city, destroy property, and murder many of the peaceable inhabitants; yet we have great reason to expect such a scene of barbarism and distress, unless means are taken to prevent it; therefore, if Torpedoes should prevent such acts of violence, the invention must be humane.

When a fortress is besieged, and a mine driven under the citadel, the powder laid, and the train ready to light, it is the custom for the besiegers to send to the commander of the besieged, to inform him of the preparations, and leave it to his judgment to surrender or risque the explosion; if he will not surrender after such warning, and he, with his men, should be blown up, he is to be charged with the inhumanity, and not the besiegers. Should government adopt Torpedoes as a part of our means of defence, the Europeans will be informed of it, after which, should they send hostile ships into our ports among anchored Tor- pedoes or Torpedo boats, and such ships should be blown up, the inhumanity must be charged to them, and not to the American government or to this invention.

Having, in the preceding chapter, given details for a system of French Torpedo boats, which could command the narrow parts of the British channel, I may be accused of enmity to England and partiality to France; yet I have neither hatred nor particular attachment to any foreign country. I admire the in- genuity, industry, and good faith of the English people; I respect the arts, sciences, and amiable manners of the people of France. There is much in each of those countries which we may copy to great advantage. But my feelings are wholly attached to my country, and while I labour for her interest in this enterprise, I am happy that the liberty of the seas, which I believe can be effected, will not only benefit America; it will be an immense advantage to England, to France, and to every other nation. Convinced of this, I have viewed military marines as remains of ancient warlike habits, and an existing political disease, for which there has hitherto been no specific remedy. Satisfied in my own mind, that the Torpedoes now discovered, will be an effectual cure for so great an evil. To introduce them into practice, and prove their utility, I am of opinion, that blowing up English ships of war, or French, or American, were there no other, and the men on shore, would be humane experiments of the first importance to the United States and to mankind.

A VIEW

of the political economy of this invention.

AT the death of Queen Elizableth, in 1602, the royal navy consisted of the following vessels.

4	ships	of	40	guns.
4		of	32	
10		of	30	
2		of	20	
3		of	16	
2		of	12	
5		of	10	
3		of	8	
1		of	6	
4		of	4	
4		of	2	
Total	42		180	guns, with 3 hoys.

When equipped for sea, it carried 8376 men.

At the death of King James I. in 1765, the royal navy amounted to sixty-two sail; the money expended per annum was fifty thousand pounds sterling, equal to 222,222 dollars, 20 cents.

At the death of King William, in 1701--2, the navy consisted of

Ships of the line, including fourth rates - - - - - 123

Frigates - - - - - - - - - 46

Fire Ships - - - - - - - - - 87

Total   256

The whole navy mounting about 9300 guns, and to completely man the ships, it would take 52,000 men; the sum allowed per annum for the naay, was 1,046,397 pounds sterling, equal to 4,650,653 dollars, 30 cents. Thus, in one century, it increased in vessels and men six fold, and in expence twenty fold.

In 1801, the royal navy consisted of

192 ships of the line	
28 ships of 50 guns	
227 frigates	
181 sloops	
96 gun vessels	Principal force for combat, 760
11 gun barges	
15 bombs	
10 fire ships	
11 store ships	
8 yachts	
9 tenders	
2 advice boats	
5 armed transports	
13 Dutch hoys	
6 river barges	
1 convalescent ship	
130 hired ships and cutters.	

Total   945

Annual expence, 13,654,013 pounds sterling, equal 60,684,502 dollars, 40 cents; at present, I have not time to ascertain the exact number of men, which however amount to more than one hundred thousand.

From 1701 to 1801, the number of vessels have been increased four fold, and the expence twelve fold; the expence is now two hundred and seventy times greater than at the death of King James I. one hundred and eighty-five years ago.

State of the maritime power of nations about the year 1790.

Taken from Arnauld.

Nations.	Ships of the line.		Frigates.		Sloops.	Total Vessels.	Total Cannon.	Total Seamen.
	ships.	*guns.*		*guns.*				
Spain	72	from 112 to 58	41		109	222	10,000	50,000
Portugal	10	80 — 58	14 from 44 to 30		29	53	1,500	1,000
Naples	10	74 — 50	10		12	32	1,000	5,000
Venice	20	88 — 16	10		58	88	1,000	14,000
Ottoman Empire	30	74 — 50	50 from 50 to 10		100 galliots	180	3,000	50,000
Holland	44	74 — 56	43	40 — 24	100	187	2,300	15,000
Denmark	38	90 — 50	20	42 — 20	60 chebecks	118	3,000	12,000
Sweden	27	74 — 50	12	38 — 20	40 gallies	79	3,000	13,000
Russia	67	110 — 66	36	44 — 28	700 various	803	9,000	21,000
France	81	118 — 64	69	40 — 30	141 various	291	14,000	78,000
England	195	100 — 50	210		256	661	12,000	100,000
						2714	59,800	359,000

Taking the whole of these fleets, and estimating their expence by that of the British marine, it must amount to about twenty-six millions of pounds sterling per annum, equal to 115,555,555 dollars, 50 cents. Can we reflect on this table and not feel, in the most sensible manner, the folly of the eleven European nations, who support such establishments for their mutual oppression? Is there an American who, after viewing these horrid consequences of divided Europe and her barbarous policy, that can for a moment harbour a wish, that these happy States should be divided, and each petty government, in proportion to its resources, aug-ment its fleets and armies either for defence or to gratify a mad ambition, by depredating on its neighbours? If there be such men, they are in a state of political insanity, and the worst enemies to the American people. The humane and excellent Dean Tucker, in his work on political economy, published during the American revolution, has observed, " That the wars of Europe, for the last two hundred years, have, by the confession of all parties, really ended in the advantage of none, but to the manifest detriment of all. Suffice it to re-mark, that had each of the contending powers employed their subjects in cultivating and improving such lands as were clear of all disputed titles, instead of aiming at more extended possessions, they had consulted both their own and their people's greatness much more efficaciously, than all the victories of a Cesar or an Alexander." This important truth should be deeply impressed on the mind of every American.

But I will return to the fleets of Europe, and endeavour to point out the principal causes of the great in-crease of those engines of oppression, and from whence the wealth has arisen to support such expences. I will also shew the increasing resources which will, if science does not check it, enable England hereafter to support a marine of fifteen hundred armed ships, with as much ease as she now does seven hundred and sixty.

In 1602, the British nation could not possibly have paid for the expence of such a navy as it possessed in 1701, and in 1701, the resources of the nation were not equal to the expence of the navy of 1801. The reason is, that since 1602, the sciences have developed immense resources. Chemistry and mechanics have multiplied the produce of productive labour, and increased the riches of every nation in Europe; the commerce of China and the East-Indies has been opened; Russia and Sweden have become civilized and commercial; South America, the West India islands, and North America, have, from a few hundred persons, grown to a population of at least twenty-five millions; who have created a vast and productive commerce, of which there was no conception two centuries ago. Agriculture has every where been improved; the earth produces more for a given labour; manufactures are carried on, in various degrees of perfection, in every country and district of country, which, creating surplus wealth to pay for luxuries, returns millions of riches on so enterprising and commercial a people as the English, which, added to their own improvements in mechanism, manufactures, and agriculture, enables the government, at this day, to expend thirteen millions of pounds sterling, annually, on their marine. Yet the people in general live better, have more enjoyments, and because they have more enjoyments, they are in reality not more oppressed than the people of 1625, who paid only fifty thousand pounds to the marine. Such is the natural consequence of a general cultivation of the useful arts; but a just government and a wise people, should take care that the wealth which the useful arts give to them, should not be uselessly expended.

As imports and exports are the consequence of increased population and industry, the following will shew how the expences of the British marine have not only kept pace, but gained on her sources of wealth.

Table of British Imports, Exports, and Expence of the Marine, in pounds sterling.

In 1701.

Imports	5,869,609*l.*
Exports	7,621,053*l.*
Total	13,490,662*l.*

Expence of the Marine.

1,046,397*l.* or one thirteenth of the whole imports and exports.

In 1798.

Imports - - - - -	46,963,000*l.*
Export of British manufactures - -	33,602,000*l.*
Export of foreign goods - - -	14,387,000*l.*
Total	94,952,000*l.*

Expence of the Navy.

13,654,013*l.* or about one seventh of the total imports and exports.

In 1800, the population of the United States was estimated at 5,214,801 ; with this population, we import from England to the amount of seven millions sterling per annum, for which we pay, in direct and circuitous trade, equal seven millions, making our imports from England, and exports to pay for them, fourteen millions, or equal to one seventh of the imports and exports of England. Therefore, as it is the profits of trade which support the British marine, we pay one seventh of its whole expence, or about two millions sterling, and, in fact, support one seventh of seven hundred and sixty armed ships, equal 108. Thus we cherish an evil of which we complain, and unless we can destroy it, we must continue to nourish it.

In 1700, the population of England and Wales amounted to 5,475,544; in 1800, to 9,343,578; it did not double in the last century, notwithstanding the great increase of trade. As her population is now equal to one person for every six acres, there is a powerful check on its increase, and the rational calculation is, that it will not double, or rise to eighteen millions in the next two centuries. But the United States is doubling its population in about twenty-five years, or, for probable correctness, say in thirty years; consequently, in

1830 we shall have	-	-	10,429,602
1860	-	-	-	-	20,859,204
1890	-	-	-	-	40,718,408
1920	-	-	-	-	81,436,816

Even then, the acres of the United States will be more than ten to an individual. As our habits and customs are English, it is a reasonable calculation, that

In 30 years, we shall take from them to the amount of	14,000,000
60	-	-	-	-	-	-	28,000,000
90	-	-	-	-	-	-	56,000,000

This is more than they now send to all the world, which wealth resulting from American labour, being turned into England, will increase her resources equal to the maintenance of her present marine: for, as I before stated, if of seven millions which we now import, we furnish funds for the seventh parth of her naval expences, or say two millions. Seven is into fifty-six, the imports of ninety years hence, eight times; the United States will, therefore, furnish sixteen millions sterling per annum, to support the British marine, and enable England to double her present naval establishment: Thus we are continually aiding and supporting, the only tyranny which can oppress us, or disturb our tranquillity.

I am aware that, opposed to this statement, it will be said that we shall become manufacturers, and hereafter import, in proportion to our population, less from England; but, in a vast country like the United States, where lands are cheap, and men can easy be provided for in agricultural pursuits; it will be difficult for the manufactures to keep pace with the population. We are now much greater manufacturers than we were twenty-five years ago; yet our imports increase; the manufactures of England have augmented ten fold in the last century. Although her population has not doubled, yet her exports and imports have kept near even pace with each other. The consequence of manufactures, is to create abundance and give the means of purchasing luxuries; therefore, more persons enjoy the luxuries of fine articles. England has her manufactures established and her people taught; she has the start of all the world, which she will keep for very many years; nor can such superiority be an injury to America, or to France, or any other nation, provided the profits are not expended on a military marine to oppress them.* Then what is to be done to

* Many appear to be of opinion, that if Bonaparte could get the command of the seas, or had it in his power, he would reduce London to ashes, and destroy the arts and manufactures of England. Carthage is always cited as an example of a conqueror's vengeance. This, however, has never been my opinion, because it is not justified by any act of his life. In all the countries he has conquered, he has ever respected the sciences and useful arts; he has not burned Vienna, Berlin, or Madrid. Had he no other motive, his own fame, in a great measure, depends on the protection which he may give to the sciences. But, independent of this, I believe he well understands the benefit which Europe receives from English arts and industry; and his war is not against them,

arrest this enormous evil, this organizing system of oppression? One of three things must be done: we must have a marine of a force to be respected, or we must suffer our commerce to be as limited as the British government may think proper, and be laid under contribution; or, military marines must be destroyed, and liberty given to the seas.

What kind of a marine would obtain for us that consideration and respect which would give to our merchant ships unmolested admittance into the ports of Europe? Fifty ships of 80 guns each, and thirty thousand men, certainly could not guarantee to us such respect. Russia has a greater naval force, and dare not show a ship out of the Baltic. Yet fifty such ships would cost the United States twenty-five millions of dollars, and seven millions of dollars a year; which, added to repairs, dock-yards, arsenals, navy-boards, and agents, may be estimated at ten millions a year. But even could such a marine secure to us a reasonable liberty of commerce, America could not now bear such an expenditure; and where is the additional commerce to pay for ten millions a year, expended to protect it? Should our resources, in twenty years, enable us to support such a marine, I have shewn, that the British can augment their fleets also, and spare a force to meet us at sea. But were America to try her finances to the utmost, and establish a marine equal to fifty ships of 80 guns, it would be to us the greatest of misfortunes; for so many persons would become interested in obtaining a support from it, that, like England, we should continue adding, until our successors would find it a power superior to their liberty—one which would load them with taxes, press

but against the manner in which their profits are applied; that is, against the marine, and interference of the British government in all the concerns of the continent.

their children into senseless wars, nor leave them permission to complain. Should we ever be necessitated to have a marine of a force to be respected, such are the accumulated evils under which our posterity must suffer. But if science and energy should sweep military marines from the ocean, America will be the garden of the world—an example for Europe to imitate. When we contemplate the immense sums which are expended in European marine establishments, and calculate the infinite good which might have been done with the capital, we have to lament that man, instead of gratifying his ambition in wars and devastation, has not sought a more noble and lasting fame in promoting the arts, the sciences, and civilization.

The annual expence of the navy of Great Britain amounts to upwards of thirteen millions a year; as long as war continues, the expence will not be diminished; but taking the chance of war and peace for the succeeding twenty-five years, and estimate that the marine will cost ten millions a year, the expenditure in twenty-five years will be two hundred and fifty millions of pounds sterling. If driven to have a marine, such might be the expenditure of our successors; if we can avoid it, the capital might be expended in useful work. I will now give a short sketch of the improvements which might be made in America for such a sum.

First, twelve canals, running from the eastern and northern parts of the United States to the south, each fifteen hundred miles long, and fifty miles distant from each other, equal to eighteen thousand miles; thirty canals, running from the sea coast to the interior, each six hundred miles long and fifty miles apart, or eighteen thousand miles—total, thirty-six thousand miles, at three thousand pounds sterling a mile, amounting to one hundred and eight millions. Canals to this extent, would intersect a country fifteen hundred miles long six hundred miles wide, equal nine hundred thousand square miles, or seven hundred and fifty-six millions of acres, not an acre of which would be more than twenty-five miles from canal carriage; and which acres, allowing six to an individual, which is equal to the density of English population, or say seven, allowing for rivers, roads, and canals, would be ample space in a country which, by its improvements, must be fertile for one hundred and eight millions of inhabitants.

2d, Two thousand bridges, at thirty thousand pounds sterling each, equal	60,000,000
Two thousand and fifty public establishments for education, at forty thousand pounds sterling each - - - - - - - -	82,000,000
The canals - - - - - - - - - -	108,000,000
Total	250,000,000

The two hundred and fifty millions, raised by loan and funded at five per cent. would, if expended on a marine, lay a tax on the people of 12,500,000*l.* sterling a year, equal to 55,555,555 dollars a year, with a hoard of excise-men and tax-gatherers, to torment honest industry. But if expended on canals, the profits of transport would pay the interest, and give inconceivable advantages to the people. Such communications would facilitate every species of industry. Canals bending round the hills, would irrigate the grounds beneath, and convert them into luxuriant pasturage. They would bind a hundred millions of people in one inseparable compact—alike in habits, in language, and in interest; one homogeneous brotherhood, the most invulnerable, powerful, and respectable on earth. Say, legislators, you who direct the destinies of this great nation, shall Americans, like servile creatures of established habits, imitate European vices, or copy them because they are familiar? Shall they nourish a useless marine, lay the basis for its increase, and send it down the current of time to futurity, with all its complicated evils? Shall such a system consume our resources, deprive the earth of improvements, draw into its vortex ambitious men, divert the best talents of our country from useful works, and interest them in its support—creating non-productive labourers, who must be the consumers of the produce of the productive class, and diminish their enjoyments? Or will you search into the most hidden recesses of science, to find a means for preventing such incalculable evils? And direct the genius and resources of our country to useful improvements, to the sciences, the arts, education, the amendment of the public mind and morals. In such pursuits, lie real honour and the nation's glory; such are the labours of enlightened republicans—those who labour for the public good. Every order of things, which has a tendency to remove oppression and meliorate the condition of man, by directing his ambition to useful industry is, in effect, republican. Every system, which nourishes war and its consequent thousands of idlers and oppressors, is aristocratic in its effects, whatever may be its name. These sentiments exhibit my political creed, the object of all my exertions; and these principles, practised by Americans, will create for them a real grandeur of character, which will secure to them the respect and admiration of the civilized world.

FINIS.

Number and Nature of Ordnance for each of the Ships in the British Navy.

Rates.	Number of guns.	Number of guns of each nature.							Carronades.			
		42	32	24	18	12	9	6	32	24	18	12
1st	100	28	-	28	-	30	-	18	2	6	-	-
2d	98	-	28	-	30	40	-	-	2	-	6	-
3d {	80	-	26	-	26	-	24	}		-		-
	74	-	28	-	28	-	18	- }	2	-	6	-
	70	-	28	-	28	-	14	- }				-
	64	-	-	26	26	-	12	-	-	2	6	-
4th {	60	-	-	24	-	26	-	10	-	-	-	-
	50	-	-	22	-	22	-	6	-	6	-	6
5th {	44	-	-	-	20	22	-	6	-	-	8	-
	36	-	-	-	26	2	8	-	8	-	-	-
	32	-	-	-	-	26	-	6	-	6	-	-
6th {	28	-	-	-	-	-	24	4	-	6	-	-
	24	-	-	-	-	-	22	2	-	2	6	-
	20	-	-	-	-	-	20	-	-	-	-	8
Sloops	18	-	-	-	-	-	-	18	-	-	-	8

Dimensions of Ships, Number of Men, and Draught of Water.

Number of Guns.	Length on the Gun-deck.		Extreme Breadth.		Complement of Sailors.	Marines.	Depth of water required for each.	
	Ft.	In.	Ft.	In.	Num.	Officers.	Feet.	
110	190	0	53	0	875	1 Capt. 3 Subs	24	
100	186	0	52	0	875	Do.	24	
98	180	0	50	0	750	Do.	23	
90	177	6	49	0	750	Do.	23	
80	182	0	49	6	650	Do.	18	
74	182	0	48	7	650	Do.	18	
74	169	0	46	11	650	Do.	18	
64	160	0	44	6	650	1 Cap. 2 Subs.	18	
50	146	0	40	6	420	2 Lieutenants.	16	
44	140	9	38	8	300	1 Subaltern.	16	
38	144	0	39	0	300	Do.	16	
36	142	0	38	0	300	Do.	16	
32	126	0	35	4	300	Do.	15	
28	120	0	33	6	200	Do.	15	
24	114	7	32	3	200	Do.	15	
20	108	0	30	0	200	Do.	15	
18	110	0	29	6	125	Sergeant	13	
16	106	0	28	0	125	Do.	13	

N. B. The usual Complement of Marines is one for every gun in the ship.

Note on vessels of war of the United States.

From which a comparative estimate may be made of their expence, and the expence of armed Torpedo boats; also the degree of protection which a given sum would effect, expended in either way.

The ship Constitution.

Guns	54
First cost, dollars	302,718
Annual expence when in commission, dollars	100,000
Draft of water, feet	23

The Wasp.

Guns	18
First cost, dollars	60,000
Annual expence in commission, dollars	38,000
Draft of water, feet	_5

A Gun Boat.

First cost, fitted for sea, dollars	12,000
Annual expence in commission, dollars	11,000
Men	36
Number of gun boats of the United States	167

This Work having been published in haste, the errors of the press, and those of diction, shall be corrected in the second edition.